Summary

of

Robert M. Sapolsky's

Behave

The Biology of Humans at Our Best and Worst

by
Swift Reads

Table of Contents

Overview

Rossano
2021

Behave: The Biology of Humans at Our Best and Worst (2017) explains the numerous biological, cultural, and evolutionary factors that shape human behavior. Neurobiologist Robert M. Sapolsky uses studies from various scientific disciplines, including neurology, psychology, sociology, and anthropology, to explore why humans exhibit variable responses to both provocative and mundane situations.

To understand human behavior, a person must first understand the brain. According to a model proposed by neuroscientist Paul MacLean, the brain's functions can be organized into three metaphorical layers; each layer groups together regions of the brain with similar tasks. These figurative regions include a base layer that regulates the body's temperature, sends hunger signals, and controls automatic functions like breathing. In mammals, the second metaphorical brain layer regulates and produces emotions including disgust, anger, and happiness. The third layer of the brain is a recent product of evolution, and is most fully developed in primates. This last layer allows humans to think about themselves, to recall their childhood, to use their imagination, and to make complex decisions based on hypothetical

3

information. While these three metaphorical layers have some distinct functions, their tasks can sometimes overlap. Each layer influences the others. For example, hunger signals from the first layer can affect the second and third layers. Hunger lowers the ability to regulate emotions or think logically, making it harder to extend sympathy to a colleague or maintain calm when faced with a combative customer.

One of the most important parts of the brain's second layer, otherwise known as the limbic system, is the amygdala. The amygdala is the source of aggressive impulses; it's also where fear originates. Ordinarily, the amygdala helps humans learn how to avoid situations that result in pain, injury, or other negative outcomes. However, in the face of one or more overwhelming obstacles in life, such as poverty, childhood exposure to violence, or malnourishment, the amygdala will likely overreact to stimuli, regardless of whether a given situation is threatening. Overactive amygdalae can be observed in patients diagnosed with post-traumatic stress disorder (PTSD).

The amygdala's reaction to a given situation is mitigated by the frontal cortex. The job of the frontal cortex includes regulating emotion, imagining the future, and strategizing. The frontal cortex helps humans complete difficult necessary tasks on both large and small scales. A person either adheres to cultural restrictions or breaks them with the help of the frontal cortex. For example, it prompts a student to study when she would rather play video games, and it lets a toddler remember to cover his mouth when he coughs. The frontal cortex also helps a soldier pull the trigger and kill a target when his natural instinct runs against harming another human.

These complex interactions between the amygdala, the frontal cortex, and other regions in the brain happen the instant before an action. Moments before that action, environmental and sensory stimuli like aromas, sights, and sounds influence the brain's response. Which environmental and sensory stimuli the brain pays attention to depends in part on the hormones produced in the preceding days, which in turn are dependent on the synapses activated in the previous months or years. Adolescence, childhood, fetal development, and inherited genes can all influence human response in a given situation. The influencing factors for any action can be traced back all the way to humanity's origins. While the reasons behind a given action can be dizzyingly complex, scientists must consider all relevant components if they hope to understand what distinguishes an even-handed ruler from a tyrant, and a mass murderer from a talented military sniper. Understanding human behavior requires a multidisciplinary approach, as well as the ability to account for biological and cultural aspects that are not yet well understood.

Key Insights

1. Determining whether a behavior is good or bad ultimately depends on context.

2. Humans are predisposed toward creating social groups based on arbitrary distinctions.

3. Subliminal signals can easily and subtly influence behavior.

4. The frontal cortex does not fully develop until humans are well past their teenage years.

5. The ill effects of poverty are amplified in cultures with widespread financial and social inequality.

6. The urge to conform can lead to positive social behavior; it can also enable horrific acts.

7. Free will doesn't exist.

8. Modern humans are less violent than their ancestors. However, violent humans are able to victimize more people.

Key Insight 1

Determining whether a behavior is good or bad ultimately depends on context.

Analysis

If a police officer fires at and incapacitates a mass shooter, she'll be praised. If she shoots an unarmed man that she believes to be the mass shooter, she might be suspended or fired. In this example, the action of firing the trigger is the same, but the circumstances determine whether it's a laudable or reprehensible action. To understand why an action provokes applause or disgust, scientists must be willing to explore the conditions that influenced that action, as well as the social mores it will be judged by.

When scientists fail to consider contexts outside of their own cultures, they can project their own biases and customs onto their research subjects and reach conclusions that are inherently wrong. In *Sex at Dawn: How We Mate, Why We Stray and What It Means for Modern Relationships* (2010), authors Christopher Ryan and Cacilda Jethá explore the research of anthropologist Peggy Reeves Sanday, who studied the Minangkabau people in West Sumatra, Indonesia. Although some

nthropologists have argued that the Minangkabau
re a patriarchal society because women bring
ood to the men, Sanday's research shows that the
ndigenous people consider themselves to be
natriarchal. Women control family inheritance,
wn land, and worship a female deity. Men
ypically move into their wife's home, unlike in
atriarchal cultures. Similarly, some primatologists
ave falsely argued that bonobos are patriarchal
ecause males frequently receive sex and are able
o lounge around their habitat without worrying
bout fighting over food. Bonobos are matriarchal,
owever; females occupy authority positions and
nales face social repercussions if they sexually
lominate members of the group. Ryan and Jethá
rgue that the reason many anthropologists and
rimatologists are unable to recognize matriarchies
s because they expect them to reflect patriarchies,
vith females dominating and abusing males to
nforce their superiority. Instead, females enforce
ocial cooperation and non-violent resolutions,
neaning that males are able to live relatively
arefree lives while still occupying lower positions
1 the group's hierarchy. If scientists want to
nderstand the behavior of another culture or
nother species, they have to judge actions using
1e context that's relevant to that group, rather than
itting the contexts of their own cultures onto the
ituation.

Key Insight 2

Humans are predisposed toward creating social groups based on arbitrary distinctions.

Analysis

People will use any distinguishing feature to form groups and choose outcasts. Even people with progressive ideals have inherent biases against outgroups. Negative associations with a given outgroup can be lessened if people confront their biases and spend time seeing enemies as individuals. However, long-standing social prejudices can be difficult to abandon, especially if they are based in religion.

If opposing groups form a cooperative coalition, they may still cling to their own traditions while demonstrating acceptance of members of the outgroup they have come to know. In *Lost Connections: Uncovering the Real Causes of Depression — and the Unexpected Solutions* (2018), author Johann Hari explores how members of ideologically opposed groups came together in a Berlin housing project during the early 2010s. The housing project was mostly occupied by low-income Germans, social outcasts, and immigrants. Communists, members of the LGBT community,

nd Turkish settlers were the primary tenants of
he low-income housing found in that part of the
ity. Developers, seeing a real-estate gold mine in
he neighborhood, hiked rental rates to the point
where many of the occupants were either evicted
or forced to leave because they couldn't afford to
ive there anymore. After one elderly Turkish
woman threatened to kill herself because she was
acing eviction, the neighborhood banded together
o organize public protests and demanded that
ental rates in the housing project be frozen.
Turkish immigrants, who were religiously
onservative, were still wary of their LGBT
neighbors, but they started to get to know them as
ndividuals. Some attended protest meetings at the
neighborhood gay bar, and one Muslim woman
even delivered little cakes to the café owners that
were decorated with rainbow flags. The occupants
of the neighborhood hadn't abandoned their
deological principles, but their collective struggle
or their home superseded prejudice and even
mparted some level of tolerance.

Key Insight 3

Subliminal signals can easily and subtly influence behavior.

Analysis

Humans are susceptible to guessing information about people and situations using cues communicated subliminally. For example, if a job candidate has upright posture, maintains eye contact, and seems relaxed during interviews, an employer will intuit that job seeker is confident. If an expensive medicine is prescribed, a patient will receive the subliminal message that it works better even if the treatment is actually a placebo. Subliminal signals don't determine thoughts on a subject, but they can influence a person's response to a given stimulus.

A 2015 *Scientific American* article explains that humans have attempted to use subliminal cues to influence behavior for thousands of years. Even ancient Greek philosophers tried to manipulate people's behavior using subtle messaging. In the twentieth century, a number of advertisers embedded subliminal messages into their commercials in an attempt to increase the number of products sold. One of the first modern examples of subliminal advertising appeared in a 1943 Looney Tunes cartoon featuring Daffy Duck, during which a message reading "BUY BONDS" flashed before viewers. Subliminal messaging in advertising fell out of favor between the 1960s and 1980s because researchers were unable to prove that such messages caused audiences to buy more of a specified brand. However, research in the 1990s and 2000s showed that subliminal messaging in advertising does sometimes influence purchasing decisions, but only in specific contexts. For example, participants in one study did buy a specific brand of tea after receiving subliminal messaging, but only if they already wanted something to drink. Subliminal advertising may not directly lead to increased sales to everyone who is subjected to a given commercial, but it may subtly influence the behavior of someone who is already susceptible to the company's message. Since researchers are still learning more about how subliminal messages affect people, marketers may not be able to apply it with precision.

Key Insight 4

The frontal cortex does not fully develop until humans are well past their teenage years.

Analysis

By the teen years, a child's limbic and hormonal systems have developed to a point where they are comparable to an adult's. The frontal cortex, however, won't finish developing until halfway through the twenties. The delay in frontal cortex development explains why teenagers have less impulse control, are more likely to engage in violence, and are more likely to invent creative solutions to tough problems. United States Supreme Court justices have determined that minors who commit crimes cannot be held to the same standards as adults.

Scientists acknowledge that all adolescents are still developing their frontal cortex, and therefore are more prone to impulsive behavior, but society often treats some teenagers as if they are more mature than others. Black children, for example, are often judged more harshly or assumed to have criminal tendencies when instead they are merely demonstrating the impetuous behavior that should be expected in someone whose frontal cortex has not fully developed. White children, on the other hands, often have their misbehavior dismissed as youthful antics, something that should perhaps be extended to all developing teens. In a 2017 *New York Times* column, Harvard University professor Robin Bernstein explains that presumption of childhood innocence has its roots in white supremacy. In the mid-nineteenth century, children were often portrayed as innocent and angelic, but only when they were white. Black children, in contrast, were portrayed in advertisements and popular media as uncontrollable and impervious to pain. Modern studies have found that members of all ethnic groups view African American youth as more rebellious and destructive than other children. People widely believe that black children are more culpable for criminal behavior and have a better grasp of sexuality at an earlier age. Although all young adults have underdeveloped frontal cortices, social biases shape how teenagers are treated under the law.

Key Insight 5

The ill effects of poverty are amplified in cultures with widespread financial and social inequality.

Analysis

In humans, socioeconomic status forms social hierarchy. A person's awareness of his or her position in that hierarchy can significantly influence mental and physical health. Members of the middle class are more likely to have health problems than the upper class; impoverished people are likely to have more severe health concerns than those of the middle class. If a child is raised in a poor family and is frequently made aware that other children in the neighborhood have more money, that child is more likely to suffer from preventable diseases and mental illness.

Income inequality in the United States has only increased in the past few decades, even during the Great Recession of 2008. In a 2018 study published by the Economic Policy Institute, a left-leaning think tank, researchers explain that in the decades after the Great Depression of the 1930s, income inequality between the top 1 percent of earners and the rest of society decreased because minimum wage rates were regularly raised and unemployment levels were low. Unionization in a number of industries also gave everyday employees more bargaining power when it came to advocating for increased salaries and better benefits. Since the 1970s, however, income inequality has increased in all 50 states, with top earners accounting for half or more of income growth in nearly 20 percent of those states. Researchers argue that the growth in income inequality is caused, in part, by the dismantling of collective bargaining power across the nation, as well as by the lack of legislation addressing stagnating minimum wages, lack of access to affordable housing, and other factors that make it harder for children born to one socioeconomic class to move to another during their lifetime. Union busting efforts since the 1970s have allowed CEOs and other executives to claim a larger share of the profits while workers' salaries fail to keep up with inflation. To reverse growing income inequality and the negative health consequences that come with it, lawmakers must be willing to increase the minimum wage, strengthen public amenities and affordable housing, make higher education more affordable for average families, and put measures in place that strengthen workers' abilities to advocate for improved conditions.

Key Insight 6

The urge to conform can lead to positive social behavior; it can also enable horrific acts.

Analysis

In the 1960s at Yale University, researchers carried out the controversial Milgram obedience experiment. Participants in the study were asked to administer shocks to actors posing as a student whenever they got an answer on a test wrong. The shocks were not real, but the actors were instructed to pretend the shocks were increasingly painful. Regardless of how the student reacted, most participants continued administering punishment at the goading of researchers. While some problems with the study later emerged, the experiment showed ordinary people will commit terrible acts to conform to social expectations.

Humans seem to be predisposed to conformity at an early age. A 2014 study in the scientific journal *Psychological Science* found that even toddlers have a tendency to conform to the behavior of their peers, even when they have ideas of their own. In the study, researchers presented children, orangutans, and chimpanzees with colorful boxes that had holes at the top; dropping a ball into the ight box led to a reward. Children were given a piece of chocolate, and apes were given a peanut. After the first set of children learned which box would lead to a reward, they watched three other two-year-olds perform the same exercise. These toddlers dropped their balls into a different box twice and received chocolate each time. The first set of children were then allowed to go through the experiment again. They were given three balls, and were asked to place them in the boxes while being watched by the two-year-olds they had just observed. Dropping a ball into any one of the boxes would have rewarded the children with chocolate. When watched by their peers, the children were more likely to drop their balls into the box the second group picked instead of the one they had initially picked. Chimpanzees and orangutans, on the other hand, tended to stick with the box they had first received a treat from, rather than switching to the ones used by other apes. The researchers concluded that humans, even at early ages, were more likely than apes to worry about what their peers do, and to adjust their actions to meet social expectations.

Key Insight 7

Free will doesn't exist.

Analysis

As researchers learn more about how biological factors influence behavior, it's become clear that most if not all of a person's actions and impulses are not the product of a truly free will. Some people's genes, childhoods, and neurological makeup make them more prone to violence. Biology's influence on action does not mean that violent criminals should be set free instead of imprisoned, but it does mean that people are not fully in control of their decisions.

The implication that biology, social influence, and childhood experience may preclude free will has led to speculation that future criminals may be punished before they've even committed an offense. Numerous science fiction stories and films have depicted futures with prescient law enforcement, including Philip K. Dick's *Minority Report* (1956) and the Japanese anime television series *Psycho-Pass* (2012). However, lack of free will doesn't inherently mean that a person's future is predetermined, and it is unlikely that scientists or law enforcement officials will ever be able to perfectly predict a person's future criminal behavior based solely on biology. That's because the future cannot be perfectly predicted, as theoretical physicist Stephen Hawking explains in his posthumously published book *Brief Answers to the Big Questions* (2018). In the early nineteenth century, French scientist Pierre-Simon Laplace argued that as long as researchers knew the positions of all particles in the universe as well as their speeds at a given moment, they could predict all future and past events. However, Laplace's theory was disproved in the 1920s by German scientist Werner Heisenberg, who was able to demonstrate that it's impossible to know both the speed and the position of a particle simultaneously. Even trying to measure the position of a given particle affects its speed, and vice versa, because of the rules of quantum mechanics. Heisenberg's uncertainty principle shows that there's an inherent element of randomness in nature, meaning that the future can never be predicted with full accuracy. Just as astronomers will never be able to chart the movement of celestial bodies with absolute certainty, researchers will likely never be able to predict a person's actions and future potential based on biology alone. A person's neurology, and therefore his or her future actions, is influenced by environment and experiences. Those factors can't be perfectly predicted for the same reasons that astronomical predictions are theoretically possible but practically impossible; the necessary calculations are too complex, time-consuming, and inefficient.

Modern humans are less violent than their ancestors. However, violent humans are able to victimize more people.

Analysis

In past centuries, humans were undeniably more violent than their modern offspring. Sanctioned slave trades, for example, were more widespread. Homicide rates in all countries were higher; infanticide and domestic violence were more common as well. While modern societies have become less lethal and have banned a number of cruel practices like forced marriage and animal abuse, humans are still capable of immense devastation. The relatively few people who do have violent impulses have access to better weaponry, allowing them to kill more people quickly than in previous generations.

One example of how improved weaponry allows violent individuals to hurt more people can be seen in the frequency and scale of mass shootings in the twentieth and twenty-first centuries in the United States. A 2017 NBC News report explains that deadly incidents involving lone shooters have become more frequent since the turn of the

23

century. In 2012, nearly two dozen children were killed by a single gunman at Sandy Hook Elementary in Newtown, Connecticut. Three years later, a shooter was able to kill nearly 50 people in an LGBT nightclub in Florida. In 2017, a man in Las Vegas was able to kill nearly 60 people and injure more than 500 others using modified guns. These acts were enabled, in part, by easy access to firearms capable of shooting multiple rounds in quick succession. Mass shootings have led some gun control advocates to claim that the founders of the United States could not have imagined weapons capable of rapid fire. However, law professor and National Rifle Association instructor David Kopel explains in a 2017 *Washington Post* column that weapons capable of firing multiple rounds between reloads have existed since before the 1600s. Compared to modern machinery, these guns were expensive to produce and were only available to the obscenely wealthy. It wasn't until President James Madison and future President James Monroe prioritized weaponry improvement that multi-round firearms could be produced with the help of factory-like settings, lowering their cost and making them available to the middle class. Guns capable of firing multiple rounds may have existed when the United States was formed, but they have since become cheaper to produce and purchase. Since modern weaponry allows violent eople in any economic class to act more quickly, manufacturers may have to take those extreme individuals into consideration when creating and elling armaments.

Important People

Robert M. Sapolsky is a biology and neurology professor at Stanford University whose research has focused on baboon colonies in Kenya. His previous works include *Why Zebras Don't Get Ulcers* (1994) and *A Primate's Memoir* (2001).

Paul MacLean (1913-2007) was a neuroscientist who developed a theoretical model to explain how the brain works which is still in use today.

Author's Style

Robert M. Sapolsky readily admits to readers that the science behind humanity's behavioral tendencies, while fascinating, is endlessly complex; it can easily be manipulated by prejudice, political perspective, and scientific illiteracy. *Behave*, then, serves as a review of relevant scientific studies from a variety of disciplines. The book additionally provides the average reader with a crash course in those various sciences, as well as the debates that exist within each regarding humanity's development, temperament, and innate nature. At the end of the book, Sapolsky provides three appendices that explain the basics of neuroscience, endocrinology, and how protein works in the body. These are recommended to readers who do not have a basic grounding in biology and neuroscience.

Sapolsky makes considerable effort to translate a complex subject into understandable material, while still emphasizing that many of the findings presented in the book are hotly contested and subject to further review. Throughout the book, he presents numerous case studies to explain how factors like hormones, genes, and culture can influence behavior. He also includes illustrations and pictures that help clarify his points, and sprinkles in humor to lighten the tone. Despite his efforts to write simply, he sometimes lapses into avoidable jargon. For example, in one chapter he uses the unfamiliar term "parturition" instead of simply saying that the animal gave birth.

Behave has 17 chapters, with the subject matter divided roughly into two parts. The first half of the book examines the forces that influence human behavior before an unspecified positive or negative event. Each chapter moves gradually back in time, starting first with the instant before the event and eventually examining the influence of evolutionary traits picked up hundreds or even thousands of years before the moment in question. The second half of the book further explores themes that come up in the first half, such as how humans differentiate friend from foe and how societies decide right from wrong. An introduction, epilogue, and extensive note section are included as well.

Author's Perspective

The science behind human behavior is not free of bias; throughout history, talented researchers have used theories about human behavior to justify terrible acts including genocide and widespread oppression of outcast groups. For Sapolsky, this tendency to justify human rights violations with science stems from intense focus on one discipline to the exclusion of other theories and schools of thought. A behavioral scientist who only focuses on his specialty, for example, might not consider hormonal or genetic factors complicating his research. Sapolsky attempts to circumvent this problem by continuously reminding readers of the subject's complexity. He additionally divulges his own biases: he tends toward liberalism and pacifism, while simultaneously struggling with a pessimistic view toward humanity.

In multiple sections, Sapolsky uses the findings he explores, as well as his own research, to argue for policy reforms. He advocates for a complete overhaul or even abolishment of the criminal justice system, arguing that judges should do away with the notion of punishment while still instituting reforms that can either help criminals learn prosocial behavior or keep them separated from society if they are too dangerous to live individually. In another chapter, Sapolsky argues that while having neurological confirmation of conditions like PTSD is nice, lawmakers should not require brain scans when it comes to believing soldiers who are describing their struggles with the conditions. Ultimately, Sapolsky argues that better understanding human behavior can allow people to break down social barriers and improve how they treat themselves and each other.

Made in the USA
Coppell, TX
21 December 2020